# When God Forgets the Children

# When God Forgets the Children

Dr. Joyce Wolford

Copyright © 2005 by Dr. Joyce Wolford.

ISBN :     Softcover     1-4134-1606-3

All rights reserved. No part of this book may be reproduced or transmitted in any form or by any means, electronic or mechanical, including photocopying, recording, or by any information storage and retrieval system, without permission in writing from the copyright owner.

This book was printed in the United States of America.

**To order additional copies of this book, contact:**
Xlibris Corporation
1-888-795-4274
www.Xlibris.com
Orders@Xlibris.com

# Contents

Preface ................................................................ 11

Chapter 1 ........................................................ 15
   *Changing Attitudes*
      Growing up in the Fifties
      Peers—"Jocks"
      Parents & Teachers
      Church Leaders (Pastors)

Chapter 2 ........................................................ 22
   *Training Up vs. Bringing Up*
      Parents who "walk the walk"
      How important is "training"?
      No Compromise!

Chapter 3 ........................................................ 26
   *A Thirty Year Reunion*
      Sincere Friends
      A Wise Man
      Who influenced them?
      Hungry for love

Chapter 4 .................................................. 30
    *Early Learning*
      "Give Me A Child"
      A Missionary Lady
      Practice Prepares
      God can use the "meek"
      Jesus Loves All

Chapter 5 .................................................. 34
    *Hear the Word of The Lord*
      No Truth, No Mercy,
      No Knowledge of God
      No Private Interpretation
      "I Will Forget Thy Children"
      Who believed our report?
      Evolution neither Science nor fact

Chapter 6 .................................................. 38
    *The Lies of Satan*
      Who lied?
      Who told the truth?
      Who made the decision?
      Same lie—Different day
      Precept upon precept

Chapter 7 .................................................. 43
    *The More Excellent Way*
      A "Foolproof" Plan
      A Way That Will "Never Fail"!
      More than "love"

Chapter 8 .................................................. 48
    *God Still Speaks*
      A call at nine years old
      God wants to communicate with you
      Learning To Listen

Ready For Action
Confusion not of God
Right source for answers

**Chapter 9** .................................................. 57
*God's Unique Design*
    A Colorful Tapestry
    Here is Wisdom
    How to Stop the Violence

**Chapter 10** ................................................ 63
*Dealing with People*
    Fundamental Principles
    Bits & Pieces
    Children learn what they live

**Chapter 11** ................................................ 67
*Godly Order*
    Finding Your Purpose
    Developing Relationships
    "Self Examination"

**Chapter 12** ................................................ 71
*Renewed Mind and Spirit*
    Merging of Wills
    "Born Again"
    Spiritual Law
    Add to Your Faith

**Chapter 13** ................................................ 77
*Science & Christianity*
    "True Science" agrees with "True Christianity"
    Study to show yourself approved to God

Chapter 14 .................................................... 84
    *Bible Truth*
        Is the Bible Reliable?
        Truth will make you free

Chapter 15 .................................................... 94
    *A Solution To World Problems*
        Simplicity can be complex
        Don't listen to "scoffers"
        Jesus is the answer, now "what is the question"

*This book is dedicated to my children,
Kathy and Deanna, to my great niece Lilly,
and to the students and graduates of
Crossland Christian Bible College*

# Preface

It is my prayer that all who read this book will become more aware of the value that God sees in each one of us. Beginning with children, God instructs us to *"Train up a child in the way he(she) should go: and when he is old he will not depart from it."* (Proverbs 22:6) Teaching acceptance, prosperity and self-indulgence has overshadowed learning the ways of God. Monetary gain seems to be what many see as the blessings of God, when in reality, *"The prosperity of fools shall destroy them."* (Proverbs 1:32) God's blessings exist in the heart and soul of mankind. *"Know ye not that ye are the temple of God?"* (I Corinthians 3:16) *"The Lord is a God of knowledge,* (I Samuel 2:3) and *"The fear of the Lord is the beginning of knowledge."* (Proverbs 1:7) God's ways are not our ways, but His ways are "higher" than our ways. An example is to get knowledge and add patience, brotherly kindness and *Godly charity*, as well as wisdom. The wisdom of Hosea warns that when a people reject truth, mercy and knowledge of God, He will also reject you and He will forget your children. (Hosea 4:1) *"Repent ye therefore, and be converted, that your sins may be blotted out, when the times of refreshing shall come from the presence of the Lord."* (Acts 3:19) *"Now therefore hearken unto me, O ye children: for blessed are they that keep My ways."* (Proverbs 8:32)

Because men wanted a God that they could "see", Jesus came, God in flesh, and lived on earth. (John 1:14)

Now you can know Him and the power of His resurrection. (Philippians 3:10)

There is neither Jew nor Greek, there is neither bond nor free, there is neither male nor female: for ye are all one in Christ Jesus. (Galatians 3:28)

God did not send Jesus to condemn the world, but rather to save the world and resurrect mankind to a life without sin. (John 12:47)

People are destroyed for lack of knowledge. (Hosea 4)

Faith is a "substance" and we all have some. (Romans 12:3)

The tongue is a world of iniquity that defiles the whole body. (James 3:6)

The Bible has the answers to all questions if we will "study" and search them out. (John 5:39)

We are not instructed to "read" or "memorize", but rather to "study"! (II Timothy 2:15)

If you will look to the Word of God, you can find what is missing in your life and learn how to hold on to hope for a good life now and a wonderful life with God forever.

Chapter 1

## Changing Attitudes

As I watch the tragedies unfold in the schools of American, my mind goes back to the time when I was a young person and I wonder how and when things changed. Yes, things have changed. The children are still children, but morals, thinking and attitudes are much different than when I was growing up in the Fifties. We were typical teenagers, but attitudes were such that you didn't poke fun at people... A bigger boy didn't bully a smaller boy, (because if he did someone bigger would give him a dose of his own medicine... if you know what I mean).

Girls seldom fought and there was no such thing as a "gang" beating up on one person. That would have been considered "totally cowardly". Disputes were settled by discussion or at the very worst by muscle, and without serious violence or injury. Young people wanted justice and fairness, but they didn't feel they had to "kill" to get it.

What has happened to young people today? Who is responsible for the violence and killing? Is it peers who embarrass and make fun of others and no one cares. Is it "jocks" who bully the smaller, weaker boys and no one defends him? Is it girls who reject unpopular boys or boys who reject unpopular girls? Is it parents who are so busy with life's personal desires that they forget their responsibility to the children? Is it teachers who fail to recognize the pain that some students carry day in and day out? Is it the church leader, who fails to teach the plain truth of the word of God. Is it the politicians, who are an example of dishonesty and bad behavior? Is it our "injustice" justice system of police, attorneys and judges that are an example of "legal crime"? Actually it is all of these and yet none of these.

**Peers**: While it is true that a young person's peers are important, it is not the responsibility of peers to teach friends right from wrong. How many young people have been taught the Ten Commandments, a story preserved by Biblical tradition, tensely dramatic and has had for many centuries, a hold on popular imagination. Modern scholars may tell the story of Moses a little differently, but it is equally dramatic in the importance of the event. The example of honest patient, rigorously disciplined work offers genuine knowledge of the Scriptures, instead of ignorant surmises and interpretations based on bias and superstition.

Young people still look for *truth*, *justice* and *love*. The problem is that these things seem to be difficult to find at home, in school, in movies and videos, in society and even in the churches today.

***Popular Young People ("jocks")*** Young people have been taught to be *self-thinking*, s*elf-achieving*, *self, self, self*, instead of "do unto others as you would want them to do to you."

What is so wrong about helping each other? No matter how popular you are, or how smart you are, this "self, self" attitude will eventually turn around and bite you. True JOY is brought by remembering Jesus first, others second and yourself third.

***Parents*** Young people need parents to be role models. Some parents think they have to act like their teen-aged children or be like their child's friends. However, children have their friends. What they need is responsible parents to provide, instruction, security, and a loving home environment for them. Parents need to encourage, advise and yes, respect young people. The same Bible that tells children to obey parents *in the Lord*, also says *"parents provoke not your children to wrath, but bring them up in the nurture and admonition of the Lord"*. (Ephesians 6:4)

***Teachers*** Are teachers so overworked and underpaid that they don't care that students are in pain? They insist that children do not say a prayer in class, but cursing and foul language is accepted as "no big deal".

King David wrote that *"Even a child is known by his doings, whether his work be pure and whether it be right."* (Psalm 20:11)

*But those things which proceed out of the mouth come from the heart and defile the person.* (Matthew 15:18)

Today many consider it perfectly okay to place students on serious medication, because they are difficult to control . . . never mind the side effects that result in causing them to commit criminal acts of violence later on. (Everyone seems to be looking for the "easy way out" and many doctors and social workers enjoy the money.) Proverbs 23:13 says, *"Withhold not correction from the children."* It does not say put them on medication, because you do not have time to fool with them.

Do teachers have time to notice that some of the students need to be corrected (not embarrassed) and perhaps recognized as important individuals? With an overloaded classroom can a teacher take time to see the need of a student who is trying to be acknowledged? And if the teacher does not believe in God, how can he/she possibly teach a child to have faith in the good things of life that God created?

Does anyone ever take time to tell a child that he/she is special, or, in some cases, acknowledge that they even exist. Teachers, parents, peers and church leaders pass-the-buck by saying *"It is not my responsibility, I don't get paid to do the job of parents, teachers, church pastors, etc."* While everyone makes excuses, the children suffer, and no one seems to have the answer. And, God forbid that someone say a prayer! God forbid that the children learn to look to a God who loves them and cares about them. God forbid that children be taught that when they are sad, hurt, lonely, and feeling that no one cares, they can pray to a God that has time for them, will listen to them and understand what they are experiencing. That *might possibly, in some way, offend someone* who doesn't believe. What if it isn't *proven, scientific fact* and we wouldn't want to pray if *"everyone"* doesn't agree on *"everything"*. Maybe it would be better to teach the *"THEORY"* of evolution (which is *not* Science and it is *not* fact) and hope that we will come back in some other form, in some other life, as some other animal to try it again ???

Perhaps it would be better to cut ourselves or beat our backs bloody or fast or maybe we should just pretend that there is no Creator?

Teachers and parents may not have time to listen, but children have a Heavenly Father that is NEVER too busy to listen and they deserve an opportunity to know Him or at least hear about Him and make a quality decision. *"He that planted the ear, shall He not hear?"* (Psalm 94:9) *"Behold, the LORD'S hand is not shortened, that it cannot save; neither His ear heavy that it cannot hear."* (Isaiah 59:1)

"Come unto me all you that labor and are heavily burdened, and I will give you rest." (Matthew 11:29)

Wouldn't this teaching be better than drugs or medication?

**Church Leadership** *(Pastors)* Have the church leaders become so involved in the things of the world, and so interested in numbers and money that they have forgotten how to teach the truth from the pulpits of America?

Have Ministers neglected to tell the children what is right and what is wrong? Perhaps they don't know themselves anymore. Has the message of sin, repentance and salvation been overshadowed by *giving, building, healing,* and *prosperity*? *"Woe unto you, Scribes and Pharisees, hypocrites! For ye pay tithe of mint and anise and cummin, and have omitted the "weightier" matters of the law,* **judgment**, **mercy** *and* **faith***, these ought ye to have done. Ye blind guides, which strain at a gnat, and swallow a camel."* (Matthew 23:23)

Maybe it is time to go back to preaching and teaching the Word of God with the children in the church and eliminate some of the plays and programs that are designed to entertain the children, because the adults do not want to tolerate them. Jesus said, *"Suffer the little children and forbid them not to come unto Me."* (Matthew 19:14) Have the churches placed children in a back room program to keep them quiet while adults "play religion"? Children need to hear the truth of the word of God. They need to learn Christian principals. They need to hear that they are loved and that they are a "special creation". They also need to learn to respect God by sitting quietly and listening during the service.

**Political Leaders**—Have the leaders of America become so corrupt that even the children recognize their deceit? Can our children respect a political system, justice system and legal system that are all filled with lawyers and politicians that have been taught to lie, cheat, steal and win at any cost, including the cost of sacrificing the Godly instruction of our children. *"Woe unto you lawyers! for ye have taken away the key of knowledge: Ye entered not in yourselves, and them that were entering in ye hindered."* (Luke 11:52)

*Woe unto you doctors and lawyers, and Judges for you take away widows houses and rob children of their inheritance. You serpents, you generation of vipers, how can you escape the damnation of hell? Behold I have sent unto you prophets, wise men and scribes: some you have killed, some you have openly condemned and some you have put in prison from city to city, that upon you may come all the righteous blood shed from the blood of Abel until now. The results of your wicked deeds shall come upon this generation and your house shall be left unto you desolate!* (Matthew 23:33)

*"The time is fulfilled and the kingdom of God is at hand: repent therefore and believe the Gospel."* (Mark 1:15)

# Chapter 2

## *Training Up vs. Bringing Up*

My parents trained up six children. Three boys and three girls. You may notice the word *"trained"*. Does that mean we were disciplined by spanking? Yes! Were we abused? No! All three of my brothers were drafted and served in the military.

None were ever in serious trouble with police or school authorities. Out of six children all graduated from college, four in academic fields and two in technical fields. Were we perfect? NO! Were we subjected to criticism from peers? Yes! Did teachers recognize our pain? Not always. Were we ever rejected by girls or boys? Sometimes. Did we make mistakes? Oh yes! So what was different?

My parents were NOT religious, they were Christians. They did not "talk the talk", they "walked the walk," especially my mother.

She only told you of her faith in God when you asked, but if you asked, she could tell you plenty. I remember once when my two sisters and I were having problems in our marriages and a lady asked my mother where she went wrong in raising her daughters.

The lady said, "Your sons all seem to be good providers and responsible husbands, but your daughters have trouble, where did you go wrong with the girls?" My mother replied, "There is nothing wrong with my daughters—the problem is that I didn't train their husbands".

My parents believed that there was a distinct difference in "bringing up a child" and "training a child". A friend once made the remark that the Bible says, "bring up a child in the way it should go and when it is old it will not depart." When I disagreed with her, she became angry; however, I remembered my mother's teaching and pointed out that Proverbs 22:6 says, *"Train up a child in the way he should go and when he is old, he will not depart from it"*. (It does not say they won't get off track when they are young.)

What is the difference in raising (or bringing) a child up and training a child? The difference is the same as if you were to put a young person in the military and keep him/her for two years with no training, they would come out a little older, but with little or no change in attitude. However, train him in the rules of discipline, skill and self control and he comes out with a different, more mature outlook toward life.

My dad trained my brothers to find ways to earn a living, even when jobs were not easy to find. He taught them that honesty and hard work were honorable. My oldest daughter has a favorite story of my dad that displays his total honesty and integrity. In 1957, a flood destroyed the furnishings in several homes in our neighborhood. The Federal Government sent a representative to the area with funds to assist people, and everyone in town received money, except my dad and one man who decided because my dad was honest, he would also refuse to lie. The reason was that recipients were required to sign a statement that said you could not *survive* without Federal assistance.

My dad had lived through the Great Depression and felt it would be a lie to say that he could not "survive" and requested that the word be changed or crossed out.

Of course my mother was upset, and remarked that everyone else in town (including the church pastor) signed, but my dad refused to compromise his belief in truthfulness. A neighbor said he was so impressed to have met a truly honest man that he too refused to sign. Although the two wives were not happy, we did not receive federal assistance, but we did survive.

Almost anyone can bring a child into the world and let it grow up, but it takes a devoted, caring parent to *train* a child to be an honest individual. It takes a devoted, caring teacher to train a child to show consideration for others.

It takes a devoted, caring Pastor to train a child to be honest and "God-fearing". It takes a person who has been trained in childhood to be caring, honest, considerate and understanding of others.

Training a child is not easy, but the rewards are great. *"Lo, children are a heritage of the Lord: and the fruit of the womb is His reward."* Psalm 127:3

The purpose of training is explained in Proverbs 22:15 as follows:

> "*Foolishness is bound in the heart of a child; but the rod of correction shall drive it far from him.*"

Of course, this does not give anyone the right to beat a child. The rod of correction can be whatever works to bring a child to observance of the rules of life. A good thing to remember is simply not to reward "bad behavior."

Chapter One of the book of Proverbs encourages us *"To know wisdom and instruction; to perceive the words of understanding; to receive the instruction of wisdom, justice, judgment and equity; to give subtility to the simple, to the young man knowledge and discretion."*

# Chapter 3

## *A Thirty Year Reunion*

At my 30 year high school reunion, people called me from all over the United States. My two daughters were so impressed. They couldn't understand why my former classmates, and I were so close. I explained that as we grew up, our parents taught us that we were loved and we were not to try to be like anyone except who God made us to be. Teachers taught us that we were important and that children should appreciate our free country.

Yes, we pledged allegiance to the flag of the United States of America and gave thanks to God for all who fought and died in wars to keep America free. Yes, I still honor the flag and give God thanks for America and for freedom to worship Him.

At our thirty-third year reunion Miss Boyd, a missionary lady, was presented a special honorary award for her work. Many people stopped to thank her, but one man in particular, who was a retired engineer, proceeded to tell her that he still remembered the stories and even the little songs that she taught. She smiled warmly, looking exactly as she did when I first saw her, and said, *"That's nice Jerry, but have you accepted Jesus as your personal Savior?"* He stammered as she asked, *"Are you living a Christian life?"* He hesitated and she quickly said, *"If you are not doing what I taught then perhaps I failed."*

He respectfully said, *"Please don't feel it was you, I just haven't done what I know I should do, but I will"*. She smiled and told him that was good and that she was very proud of him. Thanks to her teaching, most of the fellows there were *gentle men.*

Pastors taught that even if you were different, you were a special creation and loved by God, your Heavenly Father.

Peers wanted to be your friend—not kill you! Most police officers were considered friends of the community and most lawyers were honorable.

Dale Carnegie wrote, *"If you would win a person to your cause, first convince him/her that you are a sincere friend. Therein is a drop of honey that catches the heart which, say what you will, is the great high road to his/her reason."*

Most of us who grew up in the fifties can remember the words, "How would you feel if you were in their shoes"? Bernard Baruch said, *"It takes a wise man to be tolerant."*

People who try to understand others are exceptional individuals, who have been "trained" by someone or some event, to feel that way. In reality, you sometimes deserve very little credit for being what you are and the people you meet deserve little credit for being who they are.

I once told a lady to tell my young daughter to write her a check out of my business account. She quickly asked if my daughter was authorized to sign a check and said if she put her daughter's name on her account that her daughter would "clean her out". She was speechless when I asked, *"Who trained your daughter?"* I am so grateful that my daughters would give to me rather than take from me. I thank God for them. I am truly blessed.

A good number of people that you will meet (both children and adults) are hungry for love and understanding. It is **you** who can give them what they need. One of my mother's favorite clichés was, *"If you would like to have friends, you must first be friendly"*.

A young man once told me that he couldn't accept the fact that the Bible said you had to "love everyone as yourself" he was surprised when I told him that the Bible didn't say love "everyone" as yourself. I explained that the "neighbor", that you were to love as yourself was not everyone and not necessarily the person next door. As I proceeded to tell him the story of the "Good Samaritan", my daughter was surprised at his attentiveness to the story, because he had said he didn't care much for religion and especially preachers. She was even more shocked a week later when she heard him telling the story to his friends at a backyard barbecue where he remarked to his friends that what I told him made sense.

When a lawyer tried to trap Jesus into a wrong answer, Jesus explained who the neighbor really was. In the tenth chapter of Luke, Jesus told the story of a man who was beaten and robbed. As he lay injured and asking for help, a Levite who was very religious saw him, but offered no help. (Didn't want to get involved). Likewise, a Priest looked, but moved to the other side of the street and did nothing to help. (Might get hurt) These are people who "talk the talk". However, a Samaritan (who professes no excessive religious order) came where the man was and had compassion on him and helped him. Jesus said, *"Which now of these three, do you think, was a neighbor to him that fell among the thieves?"* (Luke 10:25-37)

I asked the young man, which of these three he felt you should love as yourself? He replied *"That's easy, the one who helped the man"! (had compassion— showed mercy)*

Once you begin to study the Word of God, you will find that most of it is just that simple. Man may confuse the Word of God, but God is NOT the author of confusion, but of peace. (I Corinthians 14:33) Children are still hungry for love and knowledge.

# Chapter 4

## *Early Learning*

What you teach a child in his/her early years is tremendously important. One Child Psychologist said, "*Give me a child from one to five and anyone can take it.*" He indicated that he could instill good character in five years that would last forever. Some people wait until a child reaches teenage years before they start to train. By then, "it may be too late"!

Elementary school years are important, but good training begins at birth. Good examples begin with parents.

My first memories of stories were "The little train that could" and "Jesus of Nazareth who went about doing good."

I heard how Daniel was brave and did not compromise what he had been taught and what he believed was right, and how David practiced for hours, days and months until the time came that he was faced with a seemingly impossible challenge and his practice and preparation enabled him to win over his much dreaded opponent. I heard the story of Moses who was embarrassed, because he had a speech impediment, and even though he was the "meekest man in the land" with low self esteem, he was chosen of God to deliver an entire nation. The story of Jesus, the divine Son of God, is that He was rejected by many, because he was humble and not considered handsome. He was betrayed by a friend, but He did not let it cause Him to hate; instead, He loved, forgave and was good to everyone. In fact He served others and taught them that they should serve each other as well. He, of course, is known as the "Great Teacher".

What is so bad about this teaching? What is so terrible about teaching the Word of God? How could we allow one nasty dishonest, uncaring woman, (who was a proven thief that believed in nothing except "self-gratification"), to influence leaders of our American schools. How could such an individual convince intelligent leaders that it is wrong to say a prayer? How could Americans who have been trained by God-fearing parents allow someone to discredit their parents and accept that Godly, moral teaching is bad? How did the leaders of a nation that was founded on the principals of trusting in God, allow the removal of prayer and rob our children and our schools of God's blessings?

It has been said that Charles Darwin, who is sometimes called the "father of the *theory* of evolution", said before he died that he was no closer to proving his "theory" than when he began. He went on to say that he found no comfort in his own *theories* as he faced his final hours. Why would you want that?

\* \* \*

One Scientist said, "*I believed in evolution, thinking that God used the process to produce higher species from lower ones, culminating in His supreme creation, which was man.*" However, during his research, he found a void that he could not dismiss. He explained, "*I could find no hard reference to a case where one species actually evolved into another species.*"

He went on to say that he contacted several institutions of higher learning and talked with several prominent people, that he felt would be able to provide the facts that he needed to prove that one species had been transmuted into another. That, of course, is not what he found.

I think we can all agree that at one time the earth was devoid of life. Also, we can agree that at some point life appeared. Now the problems begin. One of two views must be correct. Either life was spontaneously generated by accident or it was created on purpose. You can go back to a virus, but in order to reproduce it must have a living cell with protein to invade. If not a virus, maybe we could consider a single cell, the smallest being a bacterium. There are two major groups under which bacterium may be classified; 1) saprophytes, which live on dead animals and 2) parasites, which live on living animal or vegetable matter. Just as the virus must have a host cell in order to reproduce, bacteria must have a living or once living organism in order for it to survive and reproduce. Perhaps we could move on to the very complex "amoeba". An amoeba reproduces by cell division, which produces two individuals. When this happens, the chromosomes split forming two "identical" chromosomes. Whoops, there goes the theory of the natural crossing of the species.

"Cloning" and natural crossing of the species by evolution are **not** the same. However, man continues to try and find a way to "outsmart" God. "It is appointed unto man once to die, but after this the judgment." (Hebrews 9:27) Children need and deserve to know the truth! They need to prepare for life on earth and life with God forever. *"Suffer little children to come unto Me and forbid them not: for of such is the kingdom of God."* (Luke 18:16)

Chapter 5

## Hear the Word of The Lord

Hosea 4:1 says, *"Hear the word of the Lord, for the Lord hath a controversy with the inhabitants of the land, because there is no truth, no mercy, nor knowledge of God in the land. V2 By swearing, and lying, and killing, and stealing, and committing adultery, they break out, and blood toucheth blood. V3 Therefore, shall the land mourn."*

Hosea, son of Beeri, prophesied to Northern Israel during the time that Isaiah prophesied to Judah. He was a writing prophet and with a broken heart he prophesied Israel's impending exile and their restoration, when a chastened people would again acknowledge the exclusive claims of the Lord. Israel's unfaithfulness to the Lord is depicted in terms of an unfaithful wife who turned her back on a faithful husband to follow evil lovers. Although these Scriptures address the nation of Israel, we understand that God is the same today as He was yesterday. God does not change and He does not make a difference in nations and people when it comes to sinful acts. In other words, He will not excuse one nation and condemn another for the same act.

II Peter 1:20-22 says, *"Knowing this first, that no prophecy of the Scripture is of any private interpretation. For the prophecy came not by the will of man, but holy men of God spake as they were moved by the Holy Ghost."* So, the next time someone says, the Bible depends upon how you interpret it—, you can say "The Bible is *NOT* for anyone's *private interpretation*"! What God says to one, He says to ALL.

All nations, religions and people must stand before God and give an account for right and wrong doing.

Hosea 4:6 goes on to say, *"My people are destroyed for lack of knowledge: because thou hast rejected knowledge, (of God), I will also reject thee, that thou shalt be no priest to me: seeing thou has forgotten the law of thy God,* **I will also forget thy children."**

Make no mistake God does not reject children, because He is a mean God. He rejects them, because they have not been "trained" to know Him and trust Him.

"And if the blind lead the blind, both shall fall into the ditch."(Matthew 15:14) *"How shall they call on Him in whom they have not believed? And how shall they believe in Him of whom they have not heard?*

*And how shall they hear without a preacher (or teacher)? And how shall they preach, except they be sent? As it is written, how beautiful are the feet of them that preach the gospel of peace, and bring glad tidings of good things!* (Romans 10:14-15)

Isaiah said, "*But Lord, who hath believed our report?* How can you believe what you have not heard? How can you make a choice, in a matter if you have not heard both sides?

The "theory" of evolution is being taught in our public schools as "scientific fact", which is an "out-in-out lie". Evolution is neither science nor fact. It is, indeed, a religious belief that is totally without proof. Children hear this doctrine as truth without an opportunity to hear the story of creation. Is that fair? What are the evolutionists afraid of? Are the blind leading the blind? Are we looking the other way while the children are being lead into a pit?

What can we do to stop the violence and hate in our schools and in our nation? We can start by giving children a choice. We can tell them the truth. We can respect them enough to let them learn to walk in love as Christ has loved us and gave Himself for us. "*That we be no more children tossed to and fro, and carried about by every wind of doctrine.*" (Ephesians 4:14)

The Apostle Paul said, "*I count all things as nothing* (including wealth, and Pharisaical education, which he had plenty of) *for the* **excellency** *of the knowledge of Christ Jesus.*

The Apostle Paul was with the "in crowd". He socialized with kings and rulers in high places, yet he valued his relationship with Jesus above all else.

Could our children be missing something? Do you even care? If you do, it is time to let your voice be heard and put studies of creation back into public schools. *"O fools, and slow of heart to believe all that the prophets have spoken."* (Luke 24:25)

*"And He (Jesus) said unto them, These are the words which I spake unto you while I was yet with you, that all things must be fulfilled, which were written in the law of Moses, and in the prophets, and in the psalms, concerning Me."* *(Luke 24:44)*

Then opened He their understanding, that they might understand the scriptures and said unto them, *"Thus it is written and thus it behooved Christ to suffer, and to rise from the dead the third day: And that repentance and remission of sins should be preached in His name among all nations, beginning at Jerusalem; And ye are witnesses of these things."(Luke 24:46-48)*

*"Behold I send the promise of My Father upon you: but tarry ye in the city of Jerusalem, until ye be endued with power from on high."* (Luke 24:49)

# Chapter 6

## *The Lies of Satan*

During a Wednesday evening class at a church, I began my first evening of teaching by asking the children what they had learned from previous sessions and one little girl, who was about twelve years old said she knew that Satan made Adam and Eve sin, and that was why women had to have babies.

I asked if she was sure that Satan made them sin, and all the class agreed that she was correct, and that Satan caused all their problems.

I told the group if they would come back the next week I would prove to them that "Satan didn't really make them do it."

Needless to say, I got calls from a few people, including the Pastor, who had been informed of my "wrong teaching". At least it caused a few people to sit up and take notice.

When the class met the next week one of the students brought in a "religious comic book" that pictured a serpent pulling an apple off a tree and feeding it to Eve. First of all, I made her aware that a "book" cannot be compared to the King James Bible which is, in my opinion, the Word of God for today. As we studied, we agreed that God gave Adam and Eve an over abundance by giving them free access to every tree except one. He told them not to partake of the one that would harm them and that if they disobeyed His instruction they would die.

Satan told Eve that she would not surely die, but instead would become more alive than she had ever been. In fact he convinced her that she would be "like God". That sounds pretty good, doesn't it?

People still want to be like gods, but not necessarily like "the God".

I gave the young people an opportunity to decide for themselves. I asked, *"Did they die"*? The answer was YES! I asked, *"Who lied"*? The answer, *Satan*. And *"Who told the truth"*? . . . the answer, *God*! And then I asked the REALLY BIG QUESTION, *"Who made the decision"*? . . . *"Eve and Adam"*! (Genesis 3:3-4)

Believe it or not, Satan and his lies did not end with Adam and Eve. The same spirit of lies is offered to you and your children today in a somewhat different way. See if you can recognize some of the lies today:

Peers     "You can feel better and be more alive than you ever imagined; You will have

|  |  |
|---|---|
|  | more friends, more fun and your family will never know". |
| Truth | *Drugs and perverted sex will destroy relationships with friends and family and will eventually kill you!* |
| Politicians | "Separate church and state. The school is no place for God. Leave that to the home. |
| Truth | "*A child left to himself brings his mother to shame.*" (Proverbs 29:15) |
| Teachers | Evolution is science not religion. |
| Truth | *Evolution is not science, it is "theory" and it is a false religion.* |
| Parents | We can't control him. She simply will not listen. I am afraid of my own child. |
| Truth | *Who trained him/her? The results in training a child is not a "roll-of-the-dice".* |
| Pastors | Satan will make you do bad things. |
| Truth | *Satan cannot make you do anything. He can only deceive you into believing a lie, but YOU make your decision.* |

There are consistent, logical patterns of action within the reach of parents, teachers, ministers and yes, politicians, but it begins when a child is young.

"*For precept must be precept upon precept, precept upon precept, line upon line, line upon line; here a little, and there a little*". (Isaiah 28:10)

"*Because sentence is not executed speedily, the heart of the sons of man is set to do evil. But it shall not be well with the wicked, neither shall He prolong his days. When I applied my heart to know wisdom, I beheld all the work of God that a man cannot find out. Though a man labor to seek it out, yet he shall not find it; further, though a wise man think to know it, he shall not be able to find it.*" (Ecclesiastes 8)

Jesus said, "*I thank you Father, Lord of heaven and earth, because you hid things from the wise and proud and revealed them to children.*" (Matthew 11:25)

Children have a God given desire for knowledge, but adults need to help them develop their talents. Man does not have all the answers, but the Word of God does. Children need to know that they can go beyond what man knows and trust God, and they will if we give them a chance.

Paul wrote in Colossians 2:

> v2 "*That their hearts might be comforted being knit together in love, and unto all riches of the full assurance of understanding, to*

*the acknowledgment of the **mystery** of God, and of the Father, and of Christ; v3 In whom are hid all the treasures of wisdom and knowledge."*

Proverbs 2:1-5 says, *"My son, if thou wilt receive My words, and hide My commandments with thee; v2 So that thou incline thine ear unto wisdom, and apply thine heart to understanding; v3 Yea, If thou criest after knowledge, and liftest up thy voice for understanding;*
*v4 If thou seekest her as silver, and searchest for her as for hid treasures;*
*v5 Then shalt thou understand the fear of the Lord, and find the knowledge of God."*

Parents, Teachers, Pastors Lawyers, Judges, Doctors, Politicians and Children of America need to go on a "Treasure Hunt" for proof and for the truth!

*Forget not the laws of God, because length of days, long life and peace shall they add to you. Do not let **mercy** and **truth** get away from you, and you will find favor and good understanding with both God and man.* (Proverbs 3)

Chapter 7

## The More Excellent Way

One morning, I was awakened about four o'clock by the Lord. He called my name and told me to get up. I was startled and began to pray, thinking someone was in trouble. After about an hour of praying for everyone I could think of, I decided to read the Word. When I got no answer as to why I was awakened, I told the Lord that I was going to clean my kitchen as I waited to hear more. When no answer came, I became irritated at being awakened and began to doubt that I even heard anything.

Then I began to think of the time that God called Abraham (Genesis 22:1) and he said *"Here I am"*. He called Moses from a burning bush and Moses answered *"Here I am"*. God called Samuel and he answered *"Here am I"*. (I Samuel 3:4) I decided to read once more, telling the Lord that I had read it before and just as I started to give up and close the Bible, my eyes fell on the words,

*"Yet Show I Unto You A More Excellent Way."*

The words seemed to jump off the page at me and I knew that I had been awakened to read this portion of Scripture. To my surprise, I realized that this was God's "Foolproof Plan" for mankind. A Guarantee of eternal life with God." A way that the word of God says will NEVER FAIL!

You have probably heard the message many times in many different ways, but when God reveals His message, you may see it in a "new light".

It began:

*"Now concerning spiritual gifts brethren, I would not have you ignorant."* (I Cor. 12:1) Covet the best gifts, but I am going to show *YOU* "a more excellent way".

1. *"Though I speak with tongues of men and angels and have not charity—I am as a tinkling cymbal.*

    So tongues is not it!

2. *Though I have the gift of prophecy and understand all mysteries, and have not charity—It means nothing*!

    Prophesying the future is not it.

3. *And though I have so much faith that I could move mountains and have not charity, I am nothing.*

Faith even for healing is not it!

4. *Though I give all that I have to the poor, and sacrifice my body and have not charity—it will profit me nothing.*

Sacrificing your body & giving is NOT it.

What exactly is this "charity" that the Bible speaks of? Is it MORE than giving? Is it MORE than love? Is it MORE than understanding? YES! YES! YES!

If you should hear God call your name after you read this, just answer *"Here I am"* and He will take it from there.

So what is important to God? Understanding God's meaning of *charity* will answer that. Godly, charity is often referred to as "Agape love". The difference in "love" and Godly, charitable love is like comparing apples and oranges. Some want to put love in a box and pretend that gathering in church or giving to the Pastor or saying nice things is love. Others think helping the less fortunate or going out of your way to show compassion is love. Others think that being obedient is love. While many things are the offspring of love, you must search to find the treasure of God's charitable, agape love. You may want to take the test and see if you have it.

The Scriptures tell us that this charity that is a *"more excellent way"* is as follows:

1. Charity *suffers long* (is patient)
2. Godly charity *is kind*.
3. It *does not envy* others
4. Godly charity *does not try to be noticed*.
5. It *is not proud*.
6. This charity *does not brag* and act unruly.
7. It *does not ask "what's in it for me"*.
8. It is *not easily made mad*.
9. This charity *does not think evil*.
10. It *endures, believes* and *hopes* in the eternal future.
11. <u>Godly, charity *never fails*</u>!

**Are these things good for today? Yes!** You may seem a little strange to some people, but Godly, charity will still work today. The gifts of the Holy Spirit are still good for today. Tongues, prophesy, healing and giving are God's plan and they are good for all time, but they must be ministered with understanding and in conjunction with the loving charity of God to be valid.

If you passed the test, you are bound for a better place. If not—you need to "study" to show yourself approved unto God.

Children need to learn the history of the Bible. While hearts are tender, they need to know that God is pure love, and will NEVER FAIL THEM and will reward them for good behavior!

# Chapter 8

## God Still Speaks

When I was past 50 years old, I told the Lord that I appreciated Him for calling me to repentance when I was 25 years old. He answered, *"That is not when I called you."*

Then I said, "right—I thank you for calling me when I was baptized". *He answered, "That is not when I called you"*. He went on to say, *"I called you when you were nine years old, in the fourth grade of elementary school, praying just before falling asleep."*

I was astonished when I heard Him repeat my childhood prayer, word-for-word.

He went on to say that my simple, childlike prayer touched His heart and He placed a call to ministry on my life. Did I know it? No! Did I make mistakes during my high school years? Yes! Do I still make mistakes? Yes, unfortunately!

Now some will say, "I don't believe God talks to you." They will believe psychics, witchcraft, ESP, black magic, white magic, you name it and people will believe it as long as it isn't God. Why would people not believe that the one who created mankind would want to communicate with him/her? The problem is that most of us want to do the talking and have God listen and do what WE say.

We pray, "God give me this" and "God do that", and "God *if* You will do this, I will do that". How can God speak to you and communicate what is good for you if you never shut up long enough to hear Him? There are many verses of Scripture that tell us to *"be still—and hear"*.

In Numbers 9:8, Moses said, *"Stand still and I will hear what the Lord will command concerning you."* If you want to hear from God, you must learn to listen. Of course, no person has all answers to all questions, but I am convinced that we have a Heavenly Father that wants to be a part of our life. He does not ride around heaven on clouds all day. He wants to communicate with the race of mankind that He so wonderfully created in His image. Yes, every man, woman, boy and girl are "wonderfully created".

You are not an accident. You are a unique and special creation of God. Your body is made up of 60 trillion cells that join together to form basic types of tissue. These tissues, in turn, are pieced together into complex organ systems that allow the body to think, move, observe the world around it, enjoy pleasure and suffer pain. The sum total of what man knows about the human body is paled in comparison to its complexity.

Your three-pound brain coordinates its huge traffic of messages so well that an electronic computer designed to perform as efficiently would occupy a space as big as a skyscraper.

When a person performs an act, the brain signals a flash through the spinal cord to a motor nerve and from there a chemical boost jumpstarts it to trigger a muscle reaction. That, my friends, is not an accident. You are not here by "chance", you are here by "divine design".

Mans attitude toward his/her own body is decidedly ambivalent, while, at the same time, he is fascinated by it and fearful of it, partly in echo of ancient taboos and partly in the conviction that the body is too complicated to understand. The ironic thing is that what is so complicated to man is to the Creator a "piece of cake".

An estimated six billion human beings inhabit the earth, yet, by nature, not one exactly duplicates another. The circulatory system comprises some 60,000 miles of tubing, which carries blood to parts of the body. Its most impressive feature perhaps is the manner in which it keeps the blood moving away from the heart in arteries and toward the heart in veins, in spite of gravity and in spite of millions of alternative routes.

Satan, who is the father of lies, would like children to believe that this wonderful body is somehow perverted or distorted. I recently saw a public school teacher on television who is an "out-of-the-closet" homosexual man". He teaches sex education to young children, and stated that he refers young boys who have mixed feelings about sexuality to a group that assures them that it is allright to be homosexual. How many young children do you think do not have questions or mixed feelings about their sexuality? Could it be our children are being thrown into a "pit of perversion" and lies before they even have time to understand what they feel? Why is it that animals do not seem to have a problem with sexuality. They know who is male and who is female. Why? Because nature itself lets you know unless someone plants a wrong idea. *"In the beginning God created male and female and gave them dominion over the earth."*

Genesis 5:1-2 says, *"This is the book of the generations of Adam. In the day that God created man, in the likeness of God made He him; v2 Male and female created He them; and blessed them, and called their name Adam, in the day when they were created."*

Man and woman are created in the image of *God* and have the ability to procreate. This is a gift that Satan cannot duplicate. With all his power, he cannot procreate. God gave man an ability that Satan doesn't have and SATAN HATES IT! One of the ways he can stop the blessing of God toward mankind is to convince him/her that they don't know if they are male or female, or that a male can love another male or a female another female in the way that God ordained marriage between the two sexes; therefore, perverting the beauty of God's plan and diverting God's "divine order."

God's desire was that mankind be fruitful and multiply. You may note that this blessing was given "prior" to the fall. Therefore, sex as God planned it is NOT a sin.

Two men cannot multiply, nor can two women. Homosexual lifestyles are not within the blessings of God. A homosexual man is not a woman trapped in a man's body, nor is a lesbian a man trapped in a woman's body. It is, in fact, "learned behavior". Prostitution is learned behavior. Drugs and alcohol are "learned behavior". Criminal acts are "learned behavior". Although these acts may be caused by abuse, addiction or wrong teaching, they are nonetheless the result of sinful behavior or a lie of Satan, designed to destroy the beautiful creation of God.

While it is true that the body of mankind is a unique and intricate design, it is of little value without the soul (or mind). In fact, in comparison to the soul (or mind) the body is paled in design and complexity. *"For what is a man profited, if he shall gain the whole world, and lose his own soul? Or what shall a man give in exchange for his soul?"* (or mind) (Matthew 16:26)

When God breathed His breath into the nostrils of Adam, man became a *"living soul"*. Since God is eternal, this "living soul" and all of its offspring will live forever. It is a part of God and will never die. The decision that it will live forever is not yours and mine. The only decision we can make is where it will live after the death of the body that it dwells in.

Some will say, "I pray every day", but prayer is not merely what you say to God. It is responding to what God says or has already said to you. The study of God's word is an important part of your ongoing conversation and relationship with God.

Communicating with someone does not make you a part of their family. Birth or adoption is the avenue by which you become a part of a family.

What if you ask God to let you discover the interests and desires of *His* heart for a change? If you will do this sincerely, you will begin to develop confidence and know what is important to God and what He has planned for your life. You will discover the joy of understanding the good things that your Creator designed for you, and you can be "born of the Spirit of God".

In John 3:1-4 we find that, *"There was a man of the Pharisees, named Nicodemus, a ruler of the Jews :*

> V2 *The same came to Jesus by night, and said unto Him, "Rabbi, we know that Thou art a teacher come from God: for no man can do these miracles that Thou doest, except God be with him".*
>
> V3 *Jesus answered and said unto him, "Verily verily, I say unto thee, except a man be born again, he cannot see the kingdom of God".*
>
> V4 *Nicodemus saith unto Him, "How can a man be born when he is old? Can he enter the second time into the mother's womb and be born?"*

Many people cannot think beyond the natural, human, flesh and blood part of man, but there is more to man than the body. The first birth of man is natural and without decision on his/her part; however, the second birth is by choice. Jesus said in John 3:6, *"That which is born of flesh is flesh and that which is born of the Spirit is spirit."*

He went on to say do not marvel at this saying, think about the fact that the wind blows and even though you are aware of it, you don't really know where it comes from or where it goes. There are some things that man will have to accept by faith in God.

Silence and being able to wait upon the Lord are essential if you are to hear His voice.

Hearing the voice of God (though it may or may not be audible) will lead to actions.

Once you are born of the Spirit of God, you will accept responsibility for obeying the direction of God. You may be led to a friend that needs your help. You may be taken back to your past to deal with some unresolved hurt. Drastic changes may take place or you may find some small area of action. This is because our prayer is to God, who is the "Living God", and when He steps into your life with His awesome power, you may experience a dramatic and unpredictable way of responding to Him. On the other hand, He may leave you where you are for the time being. Either way, your relationship to the Lord Jesus Christ will be revealed in the unguarded moment, and that's good.

I saw a quote recently that read: *"Jesus is the answer . . . . Now what is the question?"*

You may not have answers to all questions, but you will feel safe in knowing where to go when you are confused about something.

The Bible tells us that God is *not* the author of confusion. A surgeon who was a friend to my brother Joe once told me that a good medical doctor does not always immediately remember all answers to every medical problem; however, he/she knows the best source for finding the answer quickly.

Life is a bit like the medical profession. It is too complex to always remember everything that you need to know, but you can learn the right source to go to for answers when you need them.

**Remember:** It has been said that if you ask questions, it is possible that *"something like an answer may appear."*

The problem today seems to be that children are sometimes afraid to ask questions. They are told not to talk about religion in school, or they ask for advice from the wrong people. They are afraid that parents might get upset or they don't have time to talk with you or there is something on television that you want to watch or they want to watch, or they are embarrassed to ask and the questions go unasked and the answers go unanswered, until the lack of communication and training explodes into disaster. Children need attention. They need Godly love and they need answers—and they will get them from parents, teachers, pastors or "peers". The question is who do you trust to give your children answers that will enhance their chances for success in life? ... *Think about it!*

# Chapter 9

## *God's Unique Design*

Regardless of background, I believe that a foundation in Biblical principles can help children to better understand the exciting changes that are taking place in our world.

America is one of the most complex nations in the world today, because of its diversity of people. We need to start to see the design that God has established for America and learn to weave the nation together as "One Nation Under God, with Liberty and Justice For All".

When groups segregate into races, cultures, ethnic groups, gender groups and age groups, each one becomes bland, colorless and uninteresting. Woven together people become a beautiful, colorful, diverse, unique tapestry, interlaced into God's extraordinary pattern and design. Solomon said, Here is wisdom; *"The fear of the Lord is the beginning of knowledge, but fools despise wisdom and instruction*." God did not intend for us to be comfortable in a meaningless state of "my four and no more". God wants us to be a light in the world around us, a bright candle showing forth light, the salt that preserves the earth and the people that live in it. Each and every one of us has a responsibility to God and to others. Every one of us needs wisdom in the ways of God. We need to redefine and understand what is right and what is wrong? Children need to learn that there is nothing wrong with "boundaries". From Genesis through Revelation, we can read that God established borders. I was told recently that children are no longer taught to color inside the lines on a picture, because it would prevent creativity. Therefore, there are no boundaries in the learning process anymore.

Perhaps it would be wise to teach a little less creativity and a little more about morals, respect for others and fairness. God established boundaries for the oceans and seas and said, "*Go this far and no further*". I think you would agree that this was a wise decision.

How do we find wisdom and understanding?

A quote from Ralph Waldo Emerson says:

> "Raphel paints wisdom;
> Handel sings it;
> Phidias carves it;
> Wren builds it;

Columbus sails it;
Luther preaches it;
Washington arms it;
Watt mechanizes it and
Shakespeare writes it, all in an effort to gain
   the wisdom of understanding."

A rigorous effort to bring our children back to the wisdom of Biblical *truth*, *mercy* and k*nowledge of God* should be our goal, if we want to stop the violence in our schools, our communities and our nation.

Bible teaching enables students to understand the triumphs and tribulations of human condition. It produces creative endeavors of the mind (or soul). It allows the exploration and interconnectedness of the Arts, Science, Philosophy, Literature and Theology.

The Bible teaches that mankind is a "triune being" and needs to be nourished in body, mind (soul) and spirit. Left unnourished in either one of these areas, man becomes unhealthy and out of control. Healthy persons in these three areas are more successful in understanding how, as a society, we can meet the challenge of living in harmony, protecting our environment and providing a decent standard of living for all now and for those who are to come. Make no mistake, God loves the people of the world! He created them! If negative emotions can destroy us, why is it so difficult to believe that positive emotions can heal us? The Creator of mankind wants people to be prosperous, well and happy.

Bible studies can help students to discover that dialogue and psychology is better than force in solving problems. Communication is a valuable asset in all situations.

Developing ways to solve problems and eliciting calmness and love for others is better than maintaining a "me/mine only" attitude. "Every kingdom divided against itself is brought to desolation; and every city or house divided against itself shall not stand.

If the people of America continue to divide the nation, all will come to destruction. This does not mean that everyone must agree on every issue. Biblical principles teach a down-to-earth approach to encourage expression of opinions from a "self-worth" point of view. It teaches that it is okay to disagree, even to dare to be different, and that you are not made strong by the "put down" of others, but that true strength comes from love and respect for others. It has been said that life is a perpetual act of taking a diverse body of knowledge and carving out a way in which to maneuver through this world in a meaningful and significant way.

We, parents, teachers, television and movie producers, ministers, students, friends, community, state and national leaders, need to put this into practice in any way that we can, for the good and well being of ourselves, as well as our young people. We need to think of human life on a higher plane than pleasure, money and power.

Dale Carnegie says *"The more you develop a deep, driving desire to master the principles of human life and human relations, the more you will get out of life."*

One of Mr. Carnegie's favorite expressions is, *"If you want to gather honey, don't kick over the beehive."*

Abraham Lincoln said, *"The student of today is the leader of tomorrow".*

Without Godly principles, what kind of leaders will America have in the future? We need to forget the unimportant things of life, turn off the television and learn to communicate with our children before it is too late.

You may find that communication is profitable and intriguing, and you may find that it breeds tolerance and kindness. As the clay is to the potter, so are the children of America to those in charge over them. *"The heart of the wise teaches his mouth, and adds learning to his lips."* (Proverbs 16:23)

America needs to speak the same language.

The people of America need to let the children witness their Godly communication. One language makes a people strong. Divided speech weakens a nation. *"And the whole earth was of one language and of one speech. And the Lord said,* **"Behold the people is one, and they have all one language; and now nothing will be restrained from them which they have imagined to do."** (Genesis 11)

Our founding fathers wrote, "*United we stand-Divided we fall.*" Therefore, it was decided by "majority vote" to establish America as a united, *English speaking nation.* If the American Government is going to spend tax payers money to help people coming into the United States, a priority should be to unite them by teaching the language of America, in order to establish better communications.

A multi-lingual nation is a divided nation and a divided nation is a weak nation. People coming into America need to understand the laws of the land and you cannot understand if there is no communication. There is no doubt that good communication promotes unity of thought and will help to keep the nation strong.

Behold, the people have ONE language and nothing will restrain them. That's the Word of God and that's unity!

# Chapter 10

## *Dealing with People*

There are some fundamental principals in dealing with people that perhaps, we should all consider. People are different, but some things work for most of us. Sometimes the simple things work so well that it is difficult to accept them as being of any great importance. An example is a student in a salesmanship class asked a very accomplished instructor what he felt was the most important tool in becoming successful quickly. The instructor answered, "A business card". The young, business student, felt that the answer was too simple, but most experienced people, I am sure, would agree. In dealing with people some things you may want to remember are:

1. A kind word turns away wrath.

2. A smile makes you beautiful to others.

3. *A person's name is a sweet sound to him/her.*

4. *A good listener encourages others.*

5. *Make someone feel important and you will become an important person.*

If you argue and contradict, you may achieve a victory from time to time, but it will be an empty victory, because you will never have your opponent's true friendship. *"If any man offend not in word, the same is a perfect man and able also to bridle the whole body."* (James 3:2)

This too, seems simple, but how many people do you know that never offend by words?

A Boston newspaper article read:

> "Here lies the body of William Jay,
> Who died maintaining his right of way
> He was absolutely right,
> As he sped along,
> But he's just as dead . . . .
> As if he were wrong."

Hatred is not dissolved with hatred.

Misunderstanding is never ended by argument, but by tact, diplomacy, and a willingness to try to understand another person's point of view.

Over a hundred years ago, Galileo said:

> "You cannot teach a man anything; you can only help him to find it within himself."

In reading an article titled "Bits & Pieces" the following appeared:

> "To settle an argument, both people do not need to agree, only one".
>
> "Never trust your first impression Keep calm and you may discover that your first reaction would have been your worst one".
>
> "Remember to control your temper, because you can measure the size of a person by his/her anger."
>
> "Listen to the other person. It is better to build bridges of understanding than barriers of misunderstanding".
>
> "Look for ways to agree rather than be known as the one to always disagree."
>
> "Be honest and admit mistakes, and show that you are man/woman enough to apologize."
>
> "The best way to get the best of an argument is to avoid it."

When my children were small, I found a writing as follows:

## Children Learn What The Live

IF a child lives with criticism,
    he learns to condemn
IF a child lives with hostility,
    he learns to fight
IF a child lives with ridicule,
    he learns to be shy
IF a child lives with shame,
    he learns to feel guilty

IF a child lives with tolerance,
   he learns to be patient
IF a child lives with praise,
   he learns to appreciate
IF a child lives with security
   he learns to have faith
IF a child lives with approval,
   he learns to like himself
IF a child lives with acceptance and friendship,
   he learns to find love in the world

Although this was an expression for a child's room, I hung it in an area where I could read it often, as a parent.

Children face areas of conflict that need to be addressed by parents, teachers, pastors, counselors and church leaders. They need to be assured that there is a God of creation who loves and cares about them. They need to understand that God does not love the rich more than the poor, nor the pretty more than the plain. God loves everyone the same. We are all unique and special to Him, and the children need to see and understand that kind of love.

# Chapter 11

## *Godly Order*

Scripture teaches and children need to be reassured, that each person is intricately designed according to God's plan. By consistently desiring to change ones self, is to say that God cannot be trusted.

Children need to know that there is a divine plan for their life, and that they are loved just as they are. Each and every life on earth has value and purpose. The third lecture in studies at Crossland Christian Bible College is titled "Finding Your Purpose". Most great leaders throughout history attained position by directing their God-given talents toward a definite purpose.

Both youth and adults need to clearly define goals around which they can direct activities. Scripture attaches significant benefit and reward to homes with love and harmony. Unfortunately, many parents are "out of Godly order" in the home, causing children to struggle and suffer as a result.

By out of Godly order, I do not mean that there must be a man to give orders and a wife and children as servants. Godly order is when everyone is obedient to the word of God. Absence of clearly defined moral standards for young people is resulting in acceptance of immoral activity that produces guilt, frustration and inability to think clearly about their future.

One of the most basic human needs is intimate fellowship with others. When we try to fulfill this need without knowing how to follow the freedoms and responsibilities at each level, we encounter life-long conflicts, and miss the wonderful experience of developing genuine, Godly, loving relationships.

God requires that each one of us maintain a program of "self-examination". Both young people and adults need to understand that when we have major conflicts and our spirit is grieved, we can ask God to search out the inner motives and put us back on track. God loves you and wants to communicate with you and direct or guide you. He does NOT want to boss you or control you. He gave you a mind and he wants to "train" you to use it. He does not want to merely "bring" you through life. He is a good parent who wants to share things with you.

*"Hear ye children the instruction of a Father, and attend to know understanding. For I give you good doctrine, forsake not My law."* (Proverbs 4)

*Get wisdom and understanding and they will promote you and bring you to honor. Embrace them and they will give your head an ornament of grace, and deliver a crown of glory to you.* (Proverbs 4:9)

King David was not considered important to his family, but God gave him wisdom and ability to overpower a giant in battle. The Scripture says that when David cried out in fear . . . God stood up from His throne and rescued him. What most people do not understand is that God loves you and me the same as He loved David. Of course, we know that God allowed David the position of King of Israel. While we may not be placed in the position of a king, we can know that the Bible tells us that if God is for you, He is **more** than the whole world against you! Therefore, when you are with God, you are on the "winning team"!

David said, *"I called upon the Lord and cried, and He did hear my voice out of His temple and my cries entered His ears and He arose and the earth shook and trembled. The fountains of heaven moved and shook because God was angry. There went up smoke out of His nostrils and fire out of His mouth that kindled fires that devoured everything it came too. He brought darkness and wind and clouds. He sent arrows of lightening and disturbed the waters of the sea. And He took me out and delivered me from my strong enemy and from them that hated me."*

Why would intelligent people want to keep little children from knowing a loving God such as this? David goes on to say that God will save afflicted people, but He is watching the "haughty" and He will bring them down.

Children have a Heavenly Father that will take care of their enemy. In God's eyes, an adult would be better off to have a stone tied to them and be thrown into the ocean than to harm a child.

Children have a friend whose name is *Jesus*. Someone needs to tell them the truth about Him.

# Chapter 12

## *Renewed Mind and Spirit*

When a mind (soul) is renewed and a spirit is reborn, a merging between your will and the will of God takes place. It has been said that this union produces unspeakable joy . . . the mind becomes a catalyst that holds the spirit and the body together in the will of God.

The third chapter of John tells of a man who came to Jesus and confessed that he and his friends knew that Jesus was from God, however, when Jesus told him that he had to be "born again", in order to enter the kingdom of God, he could not accept it.

Many today cannot accept the ways of God, because they are not natural. Isaiah 55:8 says, *"My thoughts are not your thoughts, neither are My ways your ways, saith the Lord. V9 For as the heavens are higher than the earth, so are My ways higher than your ways.*

God is not "natural", He is "Supernatural".

John 4:24 says, *"God is a Spirit: and they that worship Him must worship Him in spirit and in truth"*. Jesus explained that the new birth meant that you must renew your mind so that your thinking will become "spiritual" and unite with the mind of God. Jesus went on to say, "Why are you so surprised at spiritual birth? You accept the fact that the wind blows, even though you don't know where it comes from or where it goes. Why then can't you accept the fact that spiritual birth is on the same order?"

Of course you know, if you are a Bible reader that the man having the conversation with Jesus was Nicodemous, a Jewish ruler. He said, "Please explain so that I can understand." Jesus answered, *"If I told you earthly things* (the wind) *and you do not believe, how can I explain spiritual or heavenly things? That which is born of flesh is flesh,* (natural and seen with the natural eye). *That which is born of spirit is spirit"*, (supernatural and cannot be seen with the natural eye or understood with the natural mind). (John 3:7)

In other words, if you want to understand spiritual things, you must learn to think and communicate with God through your spirit.

Ephesians 5:1 tells us to be imitators of God, as children imitate their natural parents. This is not theory . . . It is "spiritual law". God never does anything without saying it first.

He is a "Faith God". God releases His faith in words and then it becomes "fact"!

While Jesus was on earth, He spoke to the sea, the wind, trees, demons and even dead people and ALL obeyed His words. Jesus said, *"He that believeth on Me, the works that I do shall he do also."* These principles of faith are based on spiritual laws and will work for anyone who will correctly apply them.

After reading and deciding to try the principles of spiritual law, I spoke to a growth on my skin and commanded it to dry up at the root in the name of Jesus Christ and in the same power that dried up the root of the fig tree when Jesus cursed it.

To my surprise, "it worked"! After I had proven this on five other skin cancers, the Holy Spirit spoke to me and asked how many it would take to make me "really believe without doubt"? Of course, I was embarrassed, because every time God removed the spot, Satan would bring a word of doubt to my mind. The word of God is true regardless of what we believe, think or say.

I recently heard a minister refer to Satan as the "seed stealer". He said we need to learn how to protect the seed that we plant until it has time to take root and grow. My brother-in-law did not believe in divine healing, but he was getting ready to go to the hospital and have a mole or lump removed from his eyelid, which had grown so large it was beginning to impair his vision. I jokingly told him that I could tell him another way to remove it and proceeded to tell him how God had performed His word for me. When I saw him again, he told me that he did as I said and cursed the lump and within three days he saw something fall as he was driving on the expressway to downtown Detroit, and it was the growth or mole that fell from his eye.

As I told this story, a friend reminded me of a young boy in my youth class that had a growth on his eyelid and we prayed and it fell off. (I had forgotten that one)

The fact is that the Word of God coupled with the power of the Holy Spirit works!

In Matthew 16:19 Jesus said, "*I give you the keys of the kingdom, whatever you bind on earth will be bound in heaven, whatever you loose on earth will be loosed in heaven.*"

"*O Lord, Thy word is settled in heaven.*" (Psalm 119:89)

A man in a wheel chair tried desperately to force himself to get up and walk. After a few minutes, I went to him and asked if he believed the word of God was true. He replied, "*I'm trying to believe, but I guess my faith is weak*". People had told him that he had to have more faith to receive the promise of God, but the word of God says you only need a little bit of faith to move a mountain. I told him that God did not promise that everything we asked would be granted, but He did say that by the stripes that Jesus suffered you *ARE* healed. I reminded him that this life is very short and if he could believe in the word of God, he would walk again, and if not in this life, he would walk in the next. Either way he would win. He agreed and left feeling victory instead of defeat.

Spoken words can program your spirit to either success or defeat. Words are containers that carry faith and doubt, and they produce after their kind. One writer said, *"Words are a scientific application of the wisdom of God applied to the psychological makeup of the soul* (or mind) *of man."*

The people of God need to begin to live in the authority of the Word of God and exercise His creative power. Would you want the negative things you say to happen, or would you rather have positive confession come to pass? If you knew that from this day forward what you say would happen exactly as you say, would you be inclined to change your vocabulary? I believe you would.

We have the divine promises of God if we would learn how and when to use them. Every prayer gives God an opportunity to communicate with us. Every act of charity opens the door for God to bless us. Every gift plants a seed that grows into a harvest.

*"Whereby are given unto us exceeding great and precious promises: that by these ye might be partakers of the divine nature, having escaped the corruption that is in the world through lust. And beside this, giving all diligence, add to your faith virtue; and to virtue knowledge; and to knowledge temperance; and to temperance patience; and to patience Godliness;*

*and to Godliness brotherly kindness; and to brotherly kindness charity, for if these things be in you, <u>and abound</u>, they make you that ye shall neither be barren nor unfruitful in the knowledge of our Lord Jesus Christ.* (II Peter 1:4-8)

Notice; the characteristices are to be more than found in you, they must <u>abound</u> in you. This means you must be <u>filled</u>, in great amount, fully supplied, if you are to partake of God's divine nature.

# Chapter 13

## *Science & Christianity*

A Nuclear Scientist, by the name of Robert Faid believed that Science and the Bible contradicted each other, and that Science was right so, he decided to study to prove once and for all that he and Science knew what they were talking about. His scholarly research; however, revealed startling facts. He was amazed to discover that "True Science" does not contradict the Bible. In fact, true science supports the Bible and the "true Bible" supports Science. The problem in many cases is that people miss what is "true" in both cases.

Faid's investigation proved the following:

1. Jesus is a historical person.

2. There is evidence for Resurrection, NOT reincarnation.

3. The Bible contains mathematical proof that the Scriptures were dictated by the Holy Spirit of God.

4. There is conclusive proof of the miracles of Jesus.

5. There is an after life, a heaven, a hell and a coming judgment.

6. Scientific evidence refutes the "theory" of evolution.

You can find more information in Dr. Faid's book titled "*A Scientific Approach To Christianity*".

Many parents and teachers will say they want *truth*, but they never stop to ask "What is truth?" Truth should be the essential business of Science. A Scientist must base conclusions on the best available evidence, as must every intelligent person, and not be too proud to change his/her position in the face of conclusive evidence to the contrary. The Bible tells us to "study" to show yourself approved unto God. I believe that anyone who will study the Word of God with an open mind will know the truth. Scripture tells us if you know the truth it will make you free. Free from what? Free from questions, doubts fables and fears. Matthew 7:7-8 says, "*Ask and you shall receive, knock and it shall be opened to you, seek and you shall find; for everyone that asks receives*; (an answer) *he that seeks, finds* (truth) *and he that knocks, it will be opened to him/her.* (understanding)

We must understand that the Holy Spirit does not force Himself on anyone. He only comes in to you by invitation. Jesus said, *"You have not because you ask not."*

No one can serve two masters. You must make a choice. Parents, teachers, ministers, community leaders and yes, children must choose. You cannot serve a "Risen Savior" and "evolution". You cannot love God and money. You cannot have good morals and teach that sin is okay. You cannot have children who respect you if you are not respectful. My mother had a cliché that she often quoted, *"Love you get free—Respect you must earn."*

You cannot have children who know the truth of God's word if you teach lies. *"Be not deceived: for God is not mocked"*, (Galatians 6:7) *and whatsoever you sow, that is what you will reap.* Whatever you give will be given back to you in good measure, pressed down and running over.

Evolutionists tell children that birds evolved from fish, and that wings of birds are adaptations of fish fins. If you examine these two appendages, you find the fin of a fish is hard and rigid, and the bones of a fish are heavy, including the structure of the spiny portion of the fin. The reason the bones of a fish are heavy is that a fish must live under water. The fish must have a specific gravity greater than water or he would float on the surface. On the other hand, the bones of a bird are hollow, including those in the wing. The bird must be light in order to fly. Therefore, just as the heavy rigid fin of the fish is engineered to push against the heavy forces of water, the wings of a bird are engineered to give strength and minimum weight for the bird to fly. There is about as much evolutionary evidence that fish evolved into birds as there is of the horse evolving into a Model-T Ford. What amazes me is that people will accept these odds over the possibility of Special Creation.

The theory of evolution tells us that life adapted itself to the environment, and that those individuals that best adapted survived while those that did not died out. If the survival of the fittest determined the type of life forms now existing in the world today, then in each species the best suited would have alone survived. We should have a bird, a fish, a reptile, a tree, a plant, etc., but we do not. There are over 625,000 different kinds of insects. There are 12,000 different species of mammals, 30,000 species of birds, 40,000 of fish, over 5,000 different species of reptiles. Why???

This tremendous variety of species of insects, birds, plants, trees, fish, reptiles and mammals makes the doctrine of natural selection and survival of the fittest quite unrealistic in the evolutionary theories when they are applied as the answer to life. The thousands of species in each category of life would have meant that an unimaginable number of mutations would have had to occur to account for the evolutionary ascent of higher life forms from lower ones.

If this were indeed responsible, each mutation would have had to be subtle enough to allow the organism to survive.

A single mutation could not have changed an amoebae into a giraffe. Millions of individual mutations would have to have occurred over a very, very long period of time, but what do we know about mutations themselves?

Science has extensively investigated mutations, which are induced by such means as radiation. Bacteria that multiply at a prodigious rate are ideally suited for this type of research. Within the time span of a month, billions of bacteria can be produced from a single parent. When bacteria are exposed to radiation, mutations do occur—many, many mutations which can be followed through countless generations.

In the end; however, regardless of the number of mutations which have been induced, there is still bacteria. Induced mutations in chickens have resulted in mutant monsters with heads and feet reversed, wings gnarled and twisted, organs drastically changed, but these mutants are still chickens.

Over ninety-nine percent of induced mutations are defects rather than improvements in the mutated organisms. When the organism still retains the power to reproduce after the mutation occurs, it has been found that the mutant-induced characteristic is regressive and becomes essentially dormant in accordance with Mendel's Laws of heredity and sexually reproducing organisms.

One of the most rigid and uncompromising laws in nature is the fixity of the species. It is the uniqueness of the chromosomes within each species which prevents the adulteration of its line. Each genus has its own kind, number, size and assortment of chromosomes, which are different from all other genera. When God assigned each species a unique set of chromosomes, in number, size, shape and configuration, He prevented the mixing of genera. Within the specific genus a fantastic variety of life occurs, with never any two individuals being exactly alike under "natural circumstances", but the genus itself has remained unchanged for as far back into the distant past as man can project. Why did God choose this design? Maybe because He is creative and didn't want His handiwork to become boring or perverted.

You and I are indeed, very special.

Just the fact that I am writing this and you are reading it makes us unique. We can reason and differentiate between cause and effect. We can question and sort out answers in pursuit of truth.

We can ponder the great mystery of life and speculate its meaning. We are masters of the earth, but we have not yet mastered ourselves. Our emotions run from heights of sublime love to pits of abject terror. We build empires that crumble and collect all manner of things, but own nothing. We are restless, and we are more than flesh, blood and bone. There exists within each of us a spark of eternity. We are special, because we are created in the image of God. An inheritance awaits us. We have but to claim it. I pray that someone will teach and convince our children of this while there is still time.

# Chapter 14

## *Bible Truth*

The Bible tells us who and what we are and what we will inherit. But how reliable is the Bible? It is accurate in geography, because Archaeologists have dug where the Bible has indicated ancient cities were and found evidence.

Historians have found the Bible to be correct. When political and cultural structures of ancient peoples are researched they are found to be right, according to Scripture. Prophecy of the Bible has been fulfilled with unexplainable accuracy.

Geologists have confirmed natural calamities spoken of in the Bible. Creation Science finds more facts in its proof than any theory it can advance. An amazing mathematical design appears throughout both the Old and New Testaments, which cannot be explained except that God put it there as proof of His authorship.

For the sake of our children, as men and women of Science and Christianity, let us put all of the misconceptions behind us and pursue the facts. Let us search for our ancestry and claim the inheritance that is meant for us.

Yes we must search. Yes, you and I are complex creatures.

Our body consists of about sixty trillion (60,000,000,000,000) cells. These cells join together to form basic types of tissue. The tissue, in turn are pieced together into complex organ systems that make the body think, move, and carry out activities with the skill of a specialist. We have four basic types of cells in our bodies; *metabolic*, *sense*, *growth* and *reproduction*. Man is the only genus who knows who we are, or for that matter cares. The "life force" may be the least understood force on earth. Two Biochemists, Vincent Sarich and Allan Wilson, decided to look for the woman who had passed the mitochondria DNA to the rest of the human race and in doing so to chart the migration of people throughout the world. This work dropped a bombshell. It devastated the work of those who attempted to explain the evolutionary assent of man through the fossil bones of lesser creatures. The work of Sarich and Wilson *speculates* the age of the woman to be older than Genesis would place her, it does; however, put her very close to the location of the Biblical Garden of Eden.

When the violent earth upheaval of the Genesis flood was taken into account, and evidence recorded, they gave this first mitochondria woman a name. They call her Eve! Isn't that a surprise?

From this work in Biochemistry, we find scientific substantiation that man originated where Genesis tells us that he did, and that he did indeed multiply and migrate to all parts of the world. This is just another example of how Science, when it has the facts straight, and the Bible—God's Word cannot possibly disagree.

Genesis 1:31 says, "*And God saw everything that He had made, and behold, it was very good.*" I submit that what chapter one of the book of Genesis has told us is historically, geologically, and scientifically accurate.

I believe that this holds true up to the third verse of chapter two, where the Bible changes from a scientific discussion to one of theology, with the discourse on spiritual rather than physical matters. Why should this change come in verse three of the second chapter? Because man, not God divided the book into chapters and verses.

Also, God is not limited to one method of creation. It is obvious that He is able to create by His spoken word or by an act of making a form. There cannot be any disagreement between the Bible and Science as long as Science has the facts and the Bible is being studied with a mind receptive to what is truly being said and not what Someone has made it into. It is only when one of these is off base that a confrontation is likely to occur.

God stamped His imprint on the words found in Genesis to let us know that it was actually God who dictated the words of Scripture. The first mention of man is written in Hebrew and is pronounced "Adam". The same word in Greek means "man" and is also pronounced "Adam".

In counting up the theomatic values of these words, it is equal to forty-six in both the Hebrew word and the Greek. This is no coincidence. God is saying to us, *"pay attention"*, this is the exact number of chromosomes found in Homo sapiens.

Mankind is immortal and there is nothing we can do to change that. God breathed life into the man that He formed from the dust of the earth and *that man* became a "living soul" (or mind). That soul (or mind) will live eternally somewhere.

The fact that the soul is eternal is not your choice or mine. The only choice we have is "where" the soul lives. You may not like it, but death is not the end of things—it is the beginning. Death for man is not peaceful, everlasting sleep, but rather a time to face judgement for our life and deeds here on earth. Jesus Christ came as evidence that the Scriptures were truly the Word of God. He said, *If you don't believe My words, believe Me for the works that I do.* In other words, if you are a "show me" person, look at the works that Jesus did.

Someone told of a young man that challenged a minister by saying, *"show me a miracle and I'll believe"*. The minister answered, *"believe and God will show you."*

The works that Jesus did and are recorded in history, should be sufficient to convince any thinking person that this man, Jesus of Nazareth, was truly what and who He claimed to be, the Son of God.

In John 14:2, Jesus said, *"In My Father's house are many mansions: if it were not true, I would have told you."* He goes on to say, *I am going to prepare a place for you and I will come back for you, so that you can be there with Me.* Thomas said, *Lord, how do we know where you are going and how to get there.* (Thomas wanted proof, just in case he had to find his own way). Jesus answered straightforward, *"I am the Way, the Truth and Life, no man comes unto the Father, but by Me."* (John 14:6) For sinful man it is impossible to return to a holy God. Through Divine Sacrifice, Jesus Christ paid the sin debt for mankind and made restitution with God for man.

We have an inheritance in heaven. Jesus spoke to the Apostle Paul and said, *"Rise and stand upon thy feet: for I have appeared unto thee for this purpose, to make thee a minister and a witness both of these things which thou hast seen, and of those things in the which I will appear unto thee; Delivering thee from the people and from the Gentiles, unto whom now I send thee: To open their eyes and to turn them from darkness to light and from the power of Satan unto God, that they may receive forgiveness of sins, and inheritance among them which are sanctified by faith that is in Me."*

Jesus says that you and I have an inheritance in heaven because of faith in Him. He also tells us when we will receive our inheritance.

When the thief on a cross believed and asked the Lord to remember him when He came into His kingdom, Jesus said, *"Verily I say unto thee today shalt thou be with Me in paradise."* (Luke 23:43)

Jesus asked the disciples, *"Who do people say that I am.* The disciples said, *Some say you are a prophet, some say you are John reincarnated or one of the prophets reincarnated.* Then Jesus asked the personal question that He asks each one of us, *"Who do YOU say that I am"*? It really doesn't matter what anyone else says or thinks. The only important issue in YOUR life is "Who do you say that Jesus is?"

In John 11:25, Jesus states clearly, *"I am the resurrection and life: He that believeth in Me, though he were dead, yet shall he live: And whosoever liveth and believeth in Me shall never die."* John 5:26,27 says, *"For as the Father hath life in Himself: so hath He given to the Son to have life in Himself; And hath given Him authority to execute judgment also, because He is the Son of man."*

Jesus is both God and man and; therefore, He is qualified to judge as both God and man. He was born into a world of sin. He was not treated well. He was not handsome, and He was lonely. The Bible tells us that He is not a God that cannot be touched by our feelings. He knows what you feel. He knows when you hurt, and yes, He cares.

I remember a time when I had injured my back by lifting. My daughter and I had moved and as I watched a Christian program on television, I talked to God about my pain.

As a matter of fact, I cried out to God in complaint. I said, "God if you expect me to do the work of a man, the least you can do is give me stronger muscles!" Do you hear me God? Do you have any idea how bad this pain is or do you even care?"

A minister on the television who was playing a piano stopped suddenly and said, "God just revealed to me that there is a lady watching this program who is in severe pain from a back injury. He has instructed me to tell you that He *does* know where you are, He understands your pain and He *does* care."

Needless to say, I was shocked by the words, but I began to move and discovered the pain had left. While I do not remember the minister's name (I think it was Pastor Hinkley), I am very aware that God spoke to me through that gentleman and healed me.

Man is looking in all directions for answers, to world problems. By the time you find the answer to one, another arises.

Matthew 22:29 says, *"Ye do err, not knowing the Scriptures, nor the power of God."*

Seek **first** the kingdom of God and His righteousness and ALL the other things will be added to you. Man is trying to put the cart before the horse and it doesn't work. Many people today, including some Christians, couldn't quote you the Ten Commandments or tell you where to find them or what they are really all about.

James 2:17 says, *"Show me your faith in God without works and I'll show you my faith by my works."* He goes on to say that without works, faith is "dead"!

God is not a God of the dead. He is the God of the living. You have an inheritance in heaven, and Jesus Christ is the way home.

Jesus is truth, He is life and He is the resurrection of the dead. Jesus said, *"I am the door"*, if you enter through me you will be saved. *"I am the Good Shepherd"* and I love and care for My sheep.

Is it possible that we can have a home in heaven just by believing in Jesus? Is it that simple? Not quite! Even the devils believe. The Bible says, you must believe "as the Scriptures have said".

How do we know what the Scriptures have said? You study. Darrell Armstrong, of the Orlando Magic said, *"If you don't know—you better ask somebody!"* Many people today say, (WWJD) What would Jesus Do? This, of course leaves the question open for you to decide. I recently told someone that I preferred to asked (WDJD). "What *did* Jesus do". No question—end of story!

It is finished!!!

There is a formula in the Bible that is a "foolproof" way to life with God after death. It is found in I Corinthians 13. All you need do is read and follow the instructions.

Yes, God has a controversy with the inhabitants of the land, but He says, "*If my people who are called by My name will humble themselves and pray, then will I hear from heaven and will heal their land.*" (2 Chronicles 7:14)

Yes, our nation is sick. Yes, we need to be healed. Proverbs 4:20-22 says, "*Attend to My words, for they are life and health to your flesh.*" God's word ministers to the total man and to the nation. Most people have used the words of their mouth to hold themselves in bondage to Satan. If you will begin to speak the Word of God from your heart, it will produce *health*, *life* and *liberty* to you.

If you have spoken negative words and established the words of the enemy in your life, you need to break that bondage and begin to establish the things that God has said are yours. Once you release the word and knowledge of God into your life, you will move to a new level of faith, you will walk in a new level of life, you will experience a new level of power through the words you speak.

Matthew 21:18-22 says, *"Now in the morning as He (Jesus) returned into the city, He hungered. V19 And when He saw a fig tree in the way, He came to it, and found nothing thereon, but leaves only,* (Here is a lesson for those who look good, but produce no fruit) *and said unto it, Let no fruit grow on thee henceforward for ever. And presently the fig three withered away. V20 And when the disciples saw it, they marveled, saying, How soon is the fig tree withered away! V21 Jesus answered and said unto them, Verily I say unto you, if ye have faith, and doubt not, ye shall not only do this which is done to the fig tree, but also if ye shall say unto this mountain, Be thou removed, and be thou cast into the sea; it shall be done. V22 And all things, whatsoever ye shall ask in prayer, believing, ye shall receive."*

Therefore, if you are not receiving what you ask God for, perhaps you are not asking in God's will or you are not asking according to God's Word.

If you and I follow instructions, He will do what He promised.

# Chapter 15

## *A Solution To World Problems*

An article in the Orlando Sentinel newspaper titled *"Ted Turner offers top literature prize,"* caught my eye and I thought back on the years that I have studied the Bible and realized that I had recently discovered a solution in ensuring the survival and prosperity of mans life on Earth.

Mr. Turner's offer was a sizeable award in dollars ($500,000) to writers for creative and possible solutions to global problems.

Unfortunately I did not win the prize, but the following was included in my answer:

> "First we must realize that simplicity can be complex and complexity simple, depending upon who is looking at the situation. For instance; my younger daughter was not doing well in a beginning Algebra class and after much coaxing, she agreed to accept help from her older sister.

Her sister, by the way, was an Architect major and had completed several courses in Geometry, Trigonometry, Calculus, etc. Therefore, what was devastatingly complex to the younger daughter was amazingly simple to the older. So it is with *"world problems"*.

If we go back to the beginning we find that Scripture tells us that *"In the beginning God created the heaven and the earth."* The same God that created all things said in the Book of James, Chapter 1, verse 5, *"If any lack wisdom, let him ask of God".* It is fascinating to watch men work and search for solutions and try to "pick each others brain", when what is so complex to man is so very simple to the One who created ALL things. Jesus asked the disciples if they understood how He raised a friend from the dead after he had been buried for three or four days. When they confessed that they did not understand, He explained that this was one of the "simple things" in the realm of the supernatural. So how do we learn to understand the things of God? According to Solomon's wisdom, *"The fear of the Lord is the beginning of knowledge"*, as recorded in Proverbs 1:7.

In order to understand this statement, we must understand the proper meaning of the word "fear". The word *fear* as it is used in this writing means to *startle, surprise* or *shock*. In other words, if something jumps out at you suddenly, it may not hurt you, but it could certainly cause "fear". Therefore, if the knowledge of God and who He is "jumps out at you", it could frighten you, but it certainly will not harm you.

The Bible says that you err for two reasons:

1) You do not know what the Scripture says (which is the book of instruction for mans survival)

2) You do not understand the power of God (which is the ability to live and perform spiritually.)

Mans "Great Mistake" is that he does not believe the Word that came from the mind of the One who created all things. What is complex to man is simple to God! But, the skeptic would say, who is God? How do you know? If He is there why can't we see Him?

Most people think of God as being a Spirit that dwells somewhere in the earth or floats around out in the universe somewhere. Remember, *"You do err, not knowing the Scripture, nor the power of God."* You see God is bigger than the universe and "all things". God does not function in the universe. God created the universe. Man may only be able to guess at the infinite, endless distance of space, but God is bigger than all that we can see or understand. The astounding revelation is that man is made in God's image and likeness. I saw a flash on a television program that showed the inner working of the human body. Usually we only see the skeletal system, the nervous system or the circulatory system, etc., but this flash showed, in color, the little specks of impurities that floated out in the fatty tissue and all the tiny, blood vessels that function strictly for the purpose of cleansing and purifying the body and suddenly, I realized that the human body functions amazingly like the universe. With everything moving and whirling and operating it's special function and if this is so, then the universe and all it's vastness also functions like God. The mind of man is structured to make choices and the body functions as designed. Man was God's creation and God enjoyed fellowship with him.

Man was placed in a tropical paradise, protected by a circle of ice that prevented interference from atmospheric impurities, such as harmful rays of the sun. He was required only to take care of his garden and food supply. Man was God's "pride and joy" and was given rule over the entire earth. He was simply instructed to believe God's word and communicate with God in the event of a question.

Unlike the individually created angels, man was designed to procreate and become a race. Genesis 5:2 says, "Male and female created He *them*: and blessed *them*, and called *their* name *Adam*, in the day when they were created."

An angel (Lucifer) created by God and established in a high ranking position in the universe, was made on a higher order than man, but without the ability to pro-create. Once he realized that man, who was less intelligent and less powerful than himself could do something that he could not do, which was to procreate, he rebelled against God and began a quest to take authority and destroy the race of man.

In order to find a solution to world problems, mankind must first recognize his enemy. God is NOT man's enemy. Jesus came (God in flesh) to defeat the power of this evil, angel and rescue man from his influence.

Satan deceived mankind by convincing them that they would be "more like God", wiser and more powerful, if they would launch out on their own and do their own thing and pay no attention to what God said or did not say. After all God gave them a mind and a free will. And look at Satan, he launched out and he was still around.

Unfortunately, man believed Satan's lie and disobeyed God and cancelled his relationship with God. In fact, Satan literally stole God's beautiful creation. Disappointed and hurt, God walked away and gave man over to Satan until he looked back and saw what Satan had done to the human race. It appears that Satan had found a way to cross the species and distort and pervert God's creation.

Out of compassion for the man that He had created in His own image, God destroyed the race of mankind with the entire planet's inhabitants and started with just a family to re-populate the Earth. He also set in motion a plan to remove the evil influence of Satan and redeem the race of man by exposing "good" and "evil" and giving man a choice in his own destiny.

Although Satan was able to somehow enter and influence the human person, he could not function in the Earth without the help and agreement of a human being. The seed of man has not been successful in crossing the human species with animal forms, but it is believed that before the flood that destroyed the earth and all existing life forms, the "supernatural powers of Satan" crossed the species and produced *monstrosities*. In other words, Satan succeeded in distorting both man and animal. According to Greek mythology, half man and half animal beings populated the earth. If this is in fact true, God did not destroy man out of hate, but out of compassion and love.

If you could think of the battle between God and Satan, as a game of chess or as war, you would see that when God made the move to send His Word into the Earth in the form of man, Satan lost the battle no matter how he moved. Had Jesus been allowed to remain on earth as a man, He would have established a kingdom for mankind by teaching, healing, and developing a proper plan of life according to God's will. By killing Jesus, He became the Sacrifice for mans sin and redeemed the race and implemented the plan of "redeemed man".

The man or woman who chooses to follow Jesus will be known throughout eternity as a part of *The*

*Resurrection Generation*, and death and Satan will never again have power over them. Jesus said, "*I have the power to lay down life and take it up again*", which He did. He also said that what He is, His followers would be like Him. All "born again" believers will be resurrected to life with Jesus Christ at the end of this time period. All of mankind born from the time of Jesus to the end of this Era, who have accepted Jesus "*as the Scriptures have said*" will re-establish the kingdom of mankind on Earth with Jesus Himself protecting the race from outside interference. The race of man will return to God's original plan, to live 1000 years and walk into eternity with God.

According to Scripture there is very little left to take place before the end of life as we know it and the new beginning of life as God has planned. I Thessalonians 5:4 says, "*But ye, brethren, are not in darkness, that that day should overtake you as a thief.*"

The following is a list of things that will let you know that the return of Jesus Christ is near:

1) "*And the Gospel shall be preached in all the world for a witness unto all nations, and then shall the end come.*" (Matthew 24:14-21)

   **Note:** Before satellites this was a hard verse to understand, now it's a piece-of-cake!

2) Luke 21:20 says, *"And when ye shall see Jerusalem compassed with armies, then know that the desolation thereof is near."*

3) II Peter 3:3 says, *"Knowing this first, that there shall come in the last days "scoffers" walking after their own lusts and saying, 'Where is the promise of the coming? For since the fathers fell asleep, all things continue as they were from the beginning of creation. For this they willingly are ignorant of, that by the word of God the heavens were of old, and the earth standing out of the water and in the water whereby the world that then was being overflowed with water perished."*

Scripture tells us that *"As it was in the day of Noah* (no one listened—some laughed and made fun, nevertheless the flood came), *so shall it be at the coming of Jesus"*.

*"They will not know* (non-believers*), but ye brethren* (believers) *will not be overtaken as a thief."*

God's people will not be taken by surprise, because they are watching and reading the signs of the time. The Bible tells us that *"The heavens will be shaken and will cast down its elements upon the Earth"*. Although prophesied hundreds of years ago, it is an easy saying to understand today, when we consider what man is doing in space.

Between mans accidental destruction and the plans of chemical or nuclear warfare, we can easily understand why God said, *"Except I shorten the days, there will be no flesh saved alive on Earth."*

There is good news; however, the same God who created all things is still alive and well able to rearrange an "out-of-control" situation. What can we do to help you ask? Can we do anything?

YES! *"If my people, who are called by My name will humble themselves and pray—then will I hear from heaven and will come and heal their land.*(II Chronicles 7:14)

Humble yourself and pray. Is that too much to ask? *"Study to show yourself approved unto God."* Is that too much to ask?

Read the Word and you may find that Jesus was not some poor little boy that had nothing. He was in fact, the Divine Son of the Living God. He was "rich", but He became poor for your sake and mine. Many of His friends were wealthy and wise. Jesus is real and history proves it.

Yes, the world operation is complex for man. Science struggles to sort it out. Men are stressed and cannot find all the answers, but to the God who created and rules the Universe, the World is "NO PROBLEM"!

To God the control of the world is a *"piece-of-cake!"*

God has no problems, He only has solutions. All man has to do is search the Scriptures. Seek and you will find. Knock and it will be opened to you.

Hear the Word of the Lord, you children of America and around the world, for the Lord has a controversy with the inhabitants of the land, because there is **no truth, nor mercy, nor knowledge of God** in the land. Seeing that you have forgotten the law of God, I will also reject you. *You will be no Priest to me and I will forget your children.*

As you were increased, so you sinned against Me: therefore, I will change your glory into shame. (Hosea 4:7) Hear the Word of the Lord and repent!

*After this I will return, and build again the tabernacle of David, which is fallen down; And I will build again the ruins thereof, and I will set it up: That the residue of men might seek after the Lord, and all the Gentiles, upon whom My name is called, saith the Lord, who doeth all these things.* (Acts 15:16, 17)

\* \* \*

Charles Darwin, by the way, was not the Father of the theory of evolution. In fact, the ideas of life forms evolving upward from lower orders are as old as human thought. The Bible tells us that *"There were times of ignorance when God winked at the beliefs of man, but now commandeth all men everywhere to repent and know the truth."* (Acts 17:30)

Evolution is a concept born of evil intentions, fostered by a mind at war with God.

II Corinthians 4:3,4 says, "*But if our Gospel be hid, it is hid to them that are lost; In whom the god of this world hath blinded the minds of them which believe not, lest the light of the glorious gospel of Christ, who is the image of God, should shine unto them.*"

Special Creation is recorded in Genesis 1:1 and we can begin there and analyze it. Our earth is one of nine planets revolving around our sun, which is a medium sized star. The distance from the Sun to Pluto, the last known planet in our solar system is approximately three trillion five hundred billion (3,500,000,000) miles. The earth revolves around the sun at a speed of 66,000 miles per hour. Our solar system is made up of nine planets and one sun, which is only a small part of another system called the Milky Way. This system is a galaxy of stars with over one hundred billion (100,000,000,000) solar systems similar to ours.

Traveling at a speed of light, or 186,000 miles per second, it would take a space ship 100,000 years to go from one side of our galaxy to the other. It is estimated that our system revolves around the core of our galaxy at approximately 481,000 miles an hour. (In other words we are flying and don't know it!). Even though our galaxy, the Milky Way, contains over one hundred billion (100,000,000,000) solar systems, it is only a small portion of a larger system called a "Super Cluster". In this Super Cluster, there are about 2,500 galaxies, with our galaxy being 40,000,000 (forty million) light years away from the core of the "Super Cluster".

Do we have an idea of how vast a "Super Cluster" is? It contains 2,500 galaxies that would take a space ship 100,000 years to cross just one. Well . . . we aren't finished! To go from the earth to the end of just the portion of the universe that we can observe, at the speed of 186,000 miles *per second* would take ten billion (10,000,000,000) years.

Did all this just happen? Can you see how the skies have become so fascinating to Scientists with Engineering skills? Is it possible that all of this just happened by chance? Evolutionists who hold to the "theory" that the universe exploded and created every living thing believe in the same odds as if you exploded a bomb in a library and discovered, when the dust settled, you had produced a completed Webster's dictionary. If this were the case, there would actually be no purpose for anything. Is that possible? I don't know about you, but I don't like those odds.

On the other hand, if the world and the universe were designed and created by an Intelligent being, then the world and the universe would have purpose and meaning.

The question to you is, "Do the children have a right to hear both possibilities, to see both sides of the coin and make their own decision?" Do the children deserve a chance to decide between chance and "special creation"?

I Samuel 2:3 says, *"Talk no more so exceeding proudly; let not arrogancy come out of your mouth: for the LORD is a God of knowledge, and by Him actions are weighed."*

Jesus had all knowledge and could have come into the world speaking as a Nuclear Scientist, a Medical Doctor, an Engineer or any number of things, but instead, He taught on a seventh grade level. Was there a reason for this? Do you think, perhaps, He wanted the children to understand Him?

Jesus said, *"Suffer the children and forbid them NOT to come unto Me!"*

Who will be held responsible for forbidding the children to say a prayer in school? Who will God hold accountable for not giving the children an opportunity to know the love of Jesus? Who will be charged with teaching the children the meaning of Truth, Mercy and Knowledge of God? Will it be Parents, Teachers, Ministers, Government Officials, Friends? I pray for God's wisdom, that you and I will not fail to do the right thing for the children.

We may not have every answer to every question, but until something better comes along, I am going to stick with the Word of God and "Special Creation", and pray for our nation, our leaders and our children.
**GOD BLESS AMERICA!**